50 Premium Waffle Cone Ice Cream Recipes

By: Kelly Johnson

Table of Contents

- Salted Caramel Pretzel
- Triple Chocolate Fudge
- Mango Sorbet
- Pistachio Crunch
- Lavender Honey
- Matcha Green Tea
- Roasted Banana with Brown Sugar
- Maple Pecan Praline
- Raspberry Cheesecake Swirl
- Strawberry Balsamic with Basil
- Espresso Mocha
- Cookie Dough Delight
- Spiced Chai Latte
- Lemon Blueberry Crumble
- Bourbon Vanilla Bean
- Cinnamon Roll Swirl
- Dark Chocolate Cherry

- Peach Melba
- Mint Chocolate Chip
- Tiramisu
- White Chocolate Raspberry Truffle
- Almond Joy
- Key Lime Pie
- Peanut Butter Cup
- Neapolitan
- Churro
- Caramelized Apple Cider
- Red Velvet Cake
- Brownie Batter
- Chocolate Hazelnut Praline
- Pineapple Coconut Sorbet
- Orange Creamsicle
- Black Forest Cake
- Coconut Macadamia
- Chocolate Peanut Butter Swirl
- S'mores

- Bourbon Caramel Pecan
- Chocolate Mint Oreo
- Watermelon Sorbet with Lime
- Cookies & Cream
- Lavender Earl Grey
- Mocha Almond Fudge
- Spumoni
- Dulce de Leche
- Mango Lime Chili
- Apple Cinnamon Streusel
- Chocolate-Covered Strawberry
- Vanilla Bourbon Pecan
- Raspberry Chocolate Chip
- Strawberry Shortcake

Salted Caramel Pretzel
Ingredients:

- 1 cup heavy cream
- 1 cup whole milk
- 3/4 cup sugar
- 1/2 cup salted caramel sauce
- 1 tsp vanilla extract
- 1/2 cup crushed pretzels

Instructions:
Heat cream, milk, and sugar in a saucepan over medium heat until sugar dissolves.
Remove from heat and stir in caramel sauce and vanilla.
Cool the mixture, then churn in an ice cream maker according to manufacturer's instructions.
Fold in crushed pretzels and freeze until firm.

Triple Chocolate Fudge

Ingredients:

- 1 cup heavy cream
- 1 cup whole milk
- 3/4 cup sugar
- 1/2 cup cocoa powder
- 4 oz dark chocolate, chopped
- 4 oz milk chocolate, chopped
- 4 oz white chocolate, chopped
- 1 tsp vanilla extract

Instructions:

Heat cream, milk, and sugar in a saucepan over medium heat until sugar dissolves.
Whisk in cocoa powder and bring to a simmer.
Remove from heat and add the chopped chocolates, stirring until melted and smooth.
Let cool, then churn in an ice cream maker.
Freeze until set.

Mango Sorbet
Ingredients:

- 4 ripe mangoes, peeled and chopped
- 1/2 cup sugar (adjust for sweetness)
- 1/2 cup water
- 1 tbsp lime juice

Instructions:
Blend mango, sugar, water, and lime juice until smooth.
Chill the mixture in the fridge for a few hours.
Churn in an ice cream maker until smooth and frozen.
Serve immediately or freeze for a firmer texture.

Pistachio Crunch

Ingredients:

- 1 cup heavy cream
- 1 cup whole milk
- 3/4 cup sugar
- 1/2 cup shelled pistachios, toasted and chopped
- 1 tsp vanilla extract
- 1/4 cup crushed honeycomb or crunchy caramel pieces

Instructions:

Heat cream, milk, and sugar in a saucepan until sugar dissolves.
Cool slightly and stir in pistachios and vanilla.
Churn in an ice cream maker until thickened, then fold in honeycomb or caramel.
Freeze until set.

Lavender Honey

Ingredients:

- 1 cup heavy cream
- 1 cup whole milk
- 3/4 cup honey
- 1 tbsp dried lavender buds
- 1 tsp vanilla extract

Instructions:
Heat cream, milk, and honey in a saucepan until hot but not boiling.
Add lavender buds and steep for about 10 minutes, then strain out the buds.
Cool, then stir in vanilla extract.
Churn in an ice cream maker until thickened and freeze until firm.

Matcha Green Tea

Ingredients:

- 1 cup heavy cream
- 1 cup whole milk
- 3/4 cup sugar
- 2 tbsp matcha powder
- 1 tsp vanilla extract

Instructions:
Heat cream, milk, and sugar until sugar dissolves.
Whisk in matcha powder until fully combined.
Cool, then churn in an ice cream maker until thickened.
Freeze until firm.

Roasted Banana with Brown Sugar

Ingredients:

- 4 ripe bananas, peeled
- 1/4 cup brown sugar
- 1 cup heavy cream
- 1 cup whole milk
- 1 tsp vanilla extract

Instructions:

Preheat oven to 375°F (190°C).
Toss bananas with brown sugar and roast for 20-25 minutes until soft and caramelized.
Puree the roasted bananas in a blender or food processor.
Mix with cream, milk, and vanilla extract, then chill.
Churn in an ice cream maker until smooth.
Freeze until set.

Maple Pecan Praline

Ingredients:

- 1 cup heavy cream
- 1 cup whole milk
- 3/4 cup maple syrup
- 1/2 cup chopped pecans, toasted
- 1 tsp vanilla extract
- 1/4 cup caramelized sugar or praline crunch pieces

Instructions:
Heat cream, milk, and maple syrup until warm.
Cool slightly, then stir in vanilla.
Churn in an ice cream maker until thickened.
Fold in toasted pecans and praline pieces.
Freeze until firm.

Raspberry Cheesecake Swirl
Ingredients:

- 1 cup heavy cream
- 1 cup whole milk
- 3/4 cup sugar
- 1/2 cup cream cheese, softened
- 1/2 cup raspberry puree
- 1 tsp vanilla extract

Instructions:
Heat cream, milk, and sugar in a saucepan until sugar dissolves.
Whisk in cream cheese until smooth and fully combined.
Cool, then churn in an ice cream maker until thickened.
Gently swirl in raspberry puree after churning and freeze until firm.

Strawberry Balsamic with Basil

Ingredients:

- 2 cups fresh strawberries, hulled and chopped
- 3/4 cup sugar
- 1 tbsp balsamic vinegar
- 1 cup heavy cream
- 1 cup whole milk
- 1/2 tsp vanilla extract
- 1/4 cup fresh basil, finely chopped

Instructions:

Blend strawberries, sugar, and balsamic vinegar until smooth.
Heat cream and milk until warm, then add vanilla extract.
Mix in the strawberry mixture and chill.
Churn in an ice cream maker. Once done, fold in fresh basil and freeze until set.

Espresso Mocha

Ingredients:

- 1 cup heavy cream
- 1 cup whole milk
- 1/2 cup sugar
- 2 tbsp cocoa powder
- 1/2 cup strong brewed espresso, cooled
- 1 tsp vanilla extract
- 1/4 cup chocolate chips

Instructions:
Whisk together cream, milk, sugar, cocoa powder, espresso, and vanilla extract.
Chill the mixture, then churn in an ice cream maker until smooth.
Fold in chocolate chips and freeze until firm.

Cookie Dough Delight
Ingredients:

- 1 cup heavy cream
- 1 cup whole milk
- 3/4 cup sugar
- 1 tsp vanilla extract
- 1/2 cup edible cookie dough (with no eggs)
- 1/4 cup mini chocolate chips

Instructions:
Combine cream, milk, sugar, and vanilla extract.
Churn the mixture in an ice cream maker until thickened.
Fold in cookie dough chunks and mini chocolate chips.
Freeze until set.

Spiced Chai Latte

Ingredients:

- 1 cup heavy cream
- 1 cup whole milk
- 1/2 cup sugar
- 2 tbsp chai tea concentrate or chai spice mix
- 1/2 tsp cinnamon
- 1/4 tsp ginger

Instructions:
Heat cream, milk, and sugar until warm.
Stir in chai concentrate or spices and mix well.
Chill, then churn in an ice cream maker.
Freeze until firm.

Lemon Blueberry Crumble
Ingredients:

- 1 cup heavy cream
- 1 cup whole milk
- 3/4 cup sugar
- 1/2 cup lemon curd
- 1/2 cup blueberry compote
- 1/4 cup graham cracker crumbs

Instructions:
Heat cream, milk, and sugar until sugar dissolves.
Stir in lemon curd and let cool.
Churn in an ice cream maker. Once done, swirl in blueberry compote and fold in graham cracker crumbs.
Freeze until firm.

Bourbon Vanilla Bean

Ingredients:

- 1 cup heavy cream
- 1 cup whole milk
- 3/4 cup sugar
- 1 vanilla bean, scraped (or 1 tbsp vanilla extract)
- 2 tbsp bourbon

Instructions:
Heat cream, milk, and sugar until sugar dissolves.
Add vanilla bean seeds (or extract) and bourbon.
Chill, then churn in an ice cream maker until thickened.
Freeze until firm.

Cinnamon Roll Swirl
 Ingredients:

- 1 cup heavy cream
- 1 cup whole milk
- 3/4 cup sugar
- 1 tsp cinnamon
- 1 tsp vanilla extract
- 1/4 cup cinnamon sugar
- 1/2 cup cream cheese (optional for creaminess)

Instructions:
Heat cream, milk, sugar, and cinnamon until sugar dissolves.
Stir in vanilla and cream cheese if using.
Churn in an ice cream maker until thickened.
Swirl in cinnamon sugar and freeze until set.

Dark Chocolate Cherry
Ingredients:

- 1 cup heavy cream
- 1 cup whole milk
- 3/4 cup sugar
- 4 oz dark chocolate, chopped
- 1/2 cup fresh or frozen cherries, pitted and chopped
- 1 tsp vanilla extract

Instructions:
Heat cream, milk, and sugar until sugar dissolves.
Add chopped dark chocolate and stir until melted and smooth.
Cool, then churn in an ice cream maker.
Once churned, fold in cherries and freeze until firm.

Peach Melba

Ingredients:

- 1 cup heavy cream
- 1 cup whole milk
- 3/4 cup sugar
- 1/2 cup peach puree
- 1/2 cup raspberry puree
- 1 tsp vanilla extract
- Fresh peach slices (for topping)

Instructions:
Whisk together cream, milk, and sugar until smooth.
Stir in peach puree and vanilla extract.
Churn in an ice cream maker. Once thickened, swirl in raspberry puree.
Serve with fresh peach slices.

Mint Chocolate Chip
Ingredients:

- 1 cup heavy cream
- 1 cup whole milk
- 3/4 cup sugar
- 1/2 tsp peppermint extract
- Green food coloring (optional)
- 1/2 cup mini chocolate chips

Instructions:
Whisk together cream, milk, and sugar until smooth.
Stir in peppermint extract and food coloring (if desired).
Churn in an ice cream maker until thickened.
Fold in mini chocolate chips and freeze until firm.

Tiramisu

Ingredients:

- 1 cup heavy cream
- 1 cup whole milk
- 3/4 cup sugar
- 1 tsp vanilla extract
- 1 tbsp instant coffee granules
- 1/4 cup coffee liqueur (optional)
- 1/4 cup mascarpone cheese
- Cocoa powder (for dusting)

Instructions:

Whisk together cream, milk, sugar, coffee granules, and vanilla until smooth.
Stir in mascarpone cheese and coffee liqueur (if using).
Churn in an ice cream maker.
Once churned, dust with cocoa powder before serving.

White Chocolate Raspberry Truffle
Ingredients:

- 1 cup heavy cream
- 1 cup whole milk
- 3/4 cup sugar
- 1/2 cup white chocolate, chopped
- 1/2 cup raspberry puree
- 1 tsp vanilla extract

Instructions:
Heat cream and milk over medium heat, then stir in sugar and white chocolate until melted and smooth.
Cool the mixture, then churn in an ice cream maker.
Swirl in raspberry puree after churning and freeze until firm.

Almond Joy
Ingredients:

- 1 cup heavy cream
- 1 cup whole milk
- 3/4 cup sugar
- 1/2 cup sweetened shredded coconut
- 1/4 cup chopped almonds
- 1/4 cup mini chocolate chips

Instructions:
Whisk together cream, milk, and sugar until smooth.
Churn in an ice cream maker until thickened.
Once done, fold in coconut, chopped almonds, and chocolate chips.
Freeze until firm.

Key Lime Pie
Ingredients:

- 1 cup heavy cream
- 1 cup whole milk
- 3/4 cup sugar
- 1/2 cup key lime juice
- 1/2 tsp vanilla extract
- 1/4 cup graham cracker crumbs (for crust)

Instructions:
Whisk together cream, milk, sugar, lime juice, and vanilla extract.
Churn in an ice cream maker.
Once done, fold in graham cracker crumbs.
Freeze until set and serve with extra graham crumbs on top.

Peanut Butter Cup

Ingredients:

- 1 cup heavy cream
- 1 cup whole milk
- 3/4 cup sugar
- 1/2 cup peanut butter
- 1/4 cup chopped peanut butter cups (for mix-ins)
- 1 tsp vanilla extract

Instructions:
Whisk together cream, milk, sugar, and peanut butter until smooth.
Churn in an ice cream maker until thickened.
Once churned, fold in chopped peanut butter cups and freeze until firm.

Neapolitan
Ingredients:

- 1 cup heavy cream
- 1 cup whole milk
- 3/4 cup sugar
- 1 tsp vanilla extract
- 2 tbsp cocoa powder
- 1/2 cup strawberry puree

Instructions:
Divide the cream mixture into three bowls.
For vanilla, keep as is and stir in vanilla extract.
For chocolate, whisk in cocoa powder until smooth.
For strawberry, fold in strawberry puree.
Churn each flavor separately, then layer them together in a container.
Freeze until firm.

Churro

Ingredients:

- 1 cup heavy cream
- 1 cup whole milk
- 3/4 cup sugar
- 1 tsp cinnamon
- 1/2 tsp vanilla extract
- Cinnamon sugar (for coating)

Instructions:
Whisk together cream, milk, sugar, cinnamon, and vanilla until smooth.
Churn in an ice cream maker until thickened.
Once done, roll the ice cream in cinnamon sugar.
Freeze until set.

Caramelized Apple Cider

Ingredients:

- 1 cup heavy cream
- 1 cup whole milk
- 3/4 cup sugar
- 1/2 cup apple cider
- 1/4 cup caramel sauce
- 1 tsp vanilla extract
- 1/2 tsp cinnamon

Instructions:
Heat cream, milk, and sugar over medium heat until sugar dissolves.
Add apple cider, caramel sauce, vanilla, and cinnamon.
Simmer for a few minutes to blend the flavors.
Chill the mixture, then churn in an ice cream maker until thickened.
Freeze until set.

Red Velvet Cake

Ingredients:

- 1 cup heavy cream
- 1 cup whole milk
- 3/4 cup sugar
- 1/4 cup red velvet cake mix (or homemade cake base)
- 1/2 tsp vanilla extract
- 1/4 cup cream cheese (optional)

Instructions:

Heat cream, milk, and sugar in a saucepan until sugar dissolves.
Whisk in red velvet cake mix (or cake crumbs from a baked red velvet cake).
Once the mixture cools, churn in an ice cream maker.
For a richer flavor, mix in cream cheese and vanilla extract before churning.
Freeze until set.

Brownie Batter

Ingredients:

- 1 cup heavy cream
- 1 cup whole milk
- 3/4 cup sugar
- 1/4 cup cocoa powder
- 1/2 cup brownie batter (raw or baked and crumbled)
- 1 tsp vanilla extract

Instructions:
Heat cream, milk, and sugar until sugar dissolves.
Add cocoa powder and vanilla extract, mixing until smooth.
Cool the mixture, then churn in an ice cream maker.
Once thickened, fold in brownie batter or crumbled brownie chunks.
Freeze until set.

Chocolate Hazelnut Praline
 Ingredients:

- 1 cup heavy cream
- 1 cup whole milk
- 3/4 cup sugar
- 2 oz dark chocolate, chopped
- 1/4 cup hazelnut spread (such as Nutella)
- 1/4 cup caramelized hazelnuts, chopped

Instructions:
Heat cream, milk, and sugar in a saucepan until sugar dissolves.
Stir in dark chocolate and hazelnut spread until smooth.
Cool the mixture, then churn in an ice cream maker.
Once churned, fold in caramelized hazelnuts.
Freeze until firm.

Pineapple Coconut Sorbet
  Ingredients:

- 2 cups fresh pineapple, chopped
- 1 cup coconut water
- 3/4 cup sugar
- 1/4 cup coconut milk
- 1 tbsp lime juice

Instructions:
Blend pineapple, coconut water, sugar, and lime juice until smooth.
Stir in coconut milk.
Chill the mixture for a few hours.
Churn in an ice cream maker until smooth and frozen.
Serve immediately or freeze until firmer.

Orange Creamsicle

Ingredients:

- 1 cup heavy cream
- 1 cup whole milk
- 3/4 cup sugar
- 1/2 cup fresh orange juice
- Zest of 1 orange
- 1 tsp vanilla extract

Instructions:
Whisk together cream, milk, sugar, orange juice, orange zest, and vanilla extract.
Chill the mixture, then churn in an ice cream maker until thickened.
Freeze until firm.

Black Forest Cake

Ingredients:

- 1 cup heavy cream
- 1 cup whole milk
- 3/4 cup sugar
- 1/4 cup cherry puree
- 1/4 cup chocolate fudge sauce
- 1/2 cup crumbled chocolate cake

Instructions:
Heat cream, milk, and sugar until sugar dissolves.
Stir in cherry puree and chocolate fudge sauce.
Cool the mixture, then churn in an ice cream maker.
Once thickened, fold in crumbled chocolate cake and freeze until set.

Coconut Macadamia

Ingredients:

- 1 cup heavy cream
- 1 cup whole milk
- 3/4 cup sugar
- 1/2 cup sweetened shredded coconut
- 1/4 cup macadamia nuts, chopped
- 1 tsp vanilla extract

Instructions:
Heat cream, milk, and sugar until sugar dissolves.
Stir in vanilla extract and shredded coconut.
Churn the mixture in an ice cream maker.
Once done, fold in chopped macadamia nuts and freeze until firm.

Chocolate Peanut Butter Swirl

Ingredients:

- 1 cup heavy cream
- 1 cup whole milk
- 3/4 cup sugar
- 1/2 cup peanut butter
- 2 oz dark chocolate, chopped
- 1 tsp vanilla extract

Instructions:
Heat cream, milk, and sugar in a saucepan until sugar dissolves.
Stir in peanut butter until smooth.
In a separate saucepan, melt dark chocolate and mix with vanilla extract.
Churn the cream mixture in an ice cream maker, then swirl in melted chocolate after churning.
Freeze until set.

S'mores

Ingredients:

- 1 cup heavy cream
- 1 cup whole milk
- 3/4 cup sugar
- 1/2 cup mini marshmallows
- 1/4 cup graham cracker crumbs
- 1/4 cup chocolate chips

Instructions:
Heat cream, milk, and sugar until sugar dissolves.
Stir in marshmallows and let them melt completely.
Chill the mixture and churn in an ice cream maker.
Once thickened, fold in graham cracker crumbs and chocolate chips.
Freeze until firm.

Bourbon Caramel Pecan

Ingredients:

- 1 cup heavy cream
- 1 cup whole milk
- 3/4 cup sugar
- 1/4 cup bourbon
- 1/2 cup caramel sauce
- 1/4 cup chopped pecans

Instructions:

Heat cream, milk, and sugar until sugar dissolves.
Stir in bourbon and caramel sauce, then simmer for a few minutes.
Cool the mixture, then churn in an ice cream maker.
Once thickened, fold in chopped pecans and freeze until set.

Chocolate Mint Oreo

Ingredients:

- 1 cup heavy cream
- 1 cup whole milk
- 3/4 cup sugar
- 1/2 tsp peppermint extract
- 1 cup Oreo cookies, chopped
- 2 oz dark chocolate, chopped

Instructions:
Whisk together cream, milk, sugar, and peppermint extract until smooth.
Churn in an ice cream maker until thickened.
Once done, fold in chopped Oreos and dark chocolate chunks.
Freeze until firm.

Watermelon Sorbet with Lime

Ingredients:

- 4 cups fresh watermelon, cubed
- 1/2 cup sugar
- 2 tbsp lime juice
- 1/4 cup lime zest

Instructions:
Blend watermelon and sugar until smooth.
Stir in lime juice and zest.
Chill the mixture, then churn in an ice cream maker until smooth and frozen.
Serve immediately or freeze until firmer.

Cookies & Cream

Ingredients:

- 1 cup heavy cream
- 1 cup whole milk
- 3/4 cup sugar
- 1 tsp vanilla extract
- 1 1/2 cups Oreo cookies, crushed

Instructions:

Whisk together cream, milk, sugar, and vanilla until smooth.
Churn in an ice cream maker until thickened.
Once done, fold in crushed Oreo cookies and freeze until firm.

Lavender Earl Grey
Ingredients:

- 1 cup heavy cream
- 1 cup whole milk
- 3/4 cup sugar
- 2 tbsp loose Earl Grey tea (or 2 tea bags)
- 1 tbsp dried lavender flowers

Instructions:
Heat cream and milk in a saucepan, then steep Earl Grey tea and lavender flowers for 5-10 minutes.
Strain out the tea and flowers, then stir in sugar.
Chill the mixture and churn in an ice cream maker.
Freeze until firm.

Mocha Almond Fudge

Ingredients:

- 1 cup heavy cream
- 1 cup whole milk
- 3/4 cup sugar
- 2 tbsp cocoa powder
- 1/2 cup brewed coffee
- 1/4 cup chocolate fudge sauce
- 1/4 cup chopped almonds

Instructions:
Whisk together cream, milk, sugar, cocoa powder, and coffee until smooth.
Heat the mixture to dissolve the cocoa powder.
Churn in an ice cream maker, then swirl in chocolate fudge sauce.
Fold in chopped almonds and freeze until firm.

Spumoni

Ingredients:

- 1 cup heavy cream
- 1 cup whole milk
- 3/4 cup sugar
- 1/2 tsp vanilla extract
- 1/4 cup maraschino cherries, chopped
- 1/4 cup pistachios, chopped
- 1/4 cup chocolate chips
- 2 tbsp cocoa powder

Instructions:
Whisk together cream, milk, sugar, and vanilla extract until smooth.
Divide the mixture into three bowls.
In one, stir in cocoa powder for the chocolate layer.
In the second, fold in maraschino cherries.
In the third, add chopped pistachios.
Churn each mixture separately in an ice cream maker, then layer them together in a container.
Freeze until firm.

Dulce de Leche

Ingredients:

- 1 cup heavy cream
- 1 cup whole milk
- 3/4 cup sugar
- 1/2 cup dulce de leche
- 1 tsp vanilla extract

Instructions:

Whisk together cream, milk, sugar, and vanilla until smooth.
Heat the mixture over medium heat until sugar dissolves.
Stir in dulce de leche until fully combined.
Chill the mixture, then churn in an ice cream maker.
Freeze until set.

Mango Lime Chili

Ingredients:

- 2 cups fresh mango, chopped
- 1 cup heavy cream
- 1 cup whole milk
- 3/4 cup sugar
- 1 tbsp lime juice
- 1/4 tsp chili powder
- 1/2 tsp cayenne pepper (optional)

Instructions:
Blend mango and sugar until smooth.
Whisk in cream, milk, lime juice, and chili powder.
Chill the mixture, then churn in an ice cream maker.
Freeze until firm. Optionally, sprinkle a little extra chili powder or cayenne on top before serving.

Apple Cinnamon Streusel

Ingredients:

- 1 cup heavy cream
- 1 cup whole milk
- 3/4 cup sugar
- 1/2 tsp cinnamon
- 1/2 cup apples, chopped
- 1/4 cup streusel topping (crumbled)

Instructions:

Heat cream, milk, sugar, and cinnamon until sugar dissolves.
Fold in chopped apples and chill the mixture.
Churn in an ice cream maker.
Once done, fold in streusel topping and freeze until set.

Chocolate-Covered Strawberry

Ingredients:

- 1 cup heavy cream
- 1 cup whole milk
- 3/4 cup sugar
- 1/2 cup strawberry puree
- 2 oz dark chocolate, chopped
- 1 tsp vanilla extract

Instructions:
Whisk together cream, milk, sugar, and vanilla extract until smooth.
Stir in strawberry puree.
Churn in an ice cream maker.
Once thickened, melt dark chocolate and drizzle over the ice cream, swirling it in.
Freeze until firm.

Vanilla Bourbon Pecan

Ingredients:

- 1 cup heavy cream
- 1 cup whole milk
- 3/4 cup sugar
- 1 tsp vanilla extract
- 1 tbsp bourbon
- 1/2 cup chopped pecans, toasted

Instructions:
Whisk together cream, milk, sugar, and vanilla extract until smooth.
Stir in bourbon and chill the mixture.
Churn in an ice cream maker.
Once churned, fold in toasted pecans and freeze until firm.

Raspberry Chocolate Chip
Ingredients:

- 1 cup heavy cream
- 1 cup whole milk
- 3/4 cup sugar
- 1/2 cup raspberry puree
- 1/2 cup mini chocolate chips
- 1 tsp vanilla extract

Instructions:
Whisk together cream, milk, sugar, and vanilla extract until smooth.
Stir in raspberry puree.
Churn in an ice cream maker.
Once done, fold in mini chocolate chips and freeze until firm.

Strawberry Shortcake

Ingredients:

- 1 cup heavy cream
- 1 cup whole milk
- 3/4 cup sugar
- 1 cup fresh strawberries, chopped
- 1/2 tsp vanilla extract
- 1/4 cup crumbled shortcake or sponge cake

Instructions:
Whisk together cream, milk, sugar, and vanilla extract until smooth.
Fold in chopped strawberries and chill the mixture.
Churn in an ice cream maker.
Once thickened, fold in crumbled shortcake and freeze until firm.